Bobbs-Merrill HEALTH FOR YOUNG AMERICA SERIES

HEALTH DAY BY DAY

by

CHARLES C. WILSON, M.D.

Former Professor of Education and Public Health
Yale University

and

ELIZABETH AVERY WILSON, Ph.D.

Former Consultant in Health Education
American Association for Health, Physical Education
and Recreation

with

ELLEN PHILBECK, Ed.S.

Assistant Professor, Health, Physical Education,
Dance, and Recreation
Radford College, Radford, Virginia

▲▲

THE BOOKS IN THIS SERIES ARE:

HEALTH AT SCHOOL

HEALTH DAY BY DAY

HEALTH AND FUN

HEALTH AND GROWTH

HEALTH AND LIVING

HEALTH AND HAPPINESS

MEN, SCIENCE AND HEALTH

HEALTH, FITNESS AND SAFETY

HEALTH DAY BY DAY

THE **BOBBS-MERRILL** COMPANY, INC.
A SUBSIDIARY OF **HOWARD W. SAMS & CO., INC.**
Publishers • INDIANAPOLIS • NEW YORK

CONTENTS

3

KEEPING WELL

LEARNING AND GROWING

TOGETHER

PHYSICAL FITNESS ACTIVITIES 166

BACK TO SCHOOL

CLOTHES FOR SCHOOL

"Summer soon will be over," said Sue
to her mother. "The first of next week
I'll start back to school. It will be
fun to go to school again."

"Yes, we must get your clothes ready
for school," said Sue's mother.

Sue and her mother looked to see
what dresses were good for school.

"These dresses are too small for me,"
said Sue. "I need some new dresses."

Sue's mother looked at the dresses
and said, "You are right. You must have
some new dresses for school."

After lunch Sue and her mother took
a bus and went downtown. They wanted
to get some new clothes for school.

Sue and Mother looked for dresses
in the stores. At last they found
two pretty dresses good for school.

Next Mother and Sue went to buy
some new shoes for school.

When Sue and her mother started home, they saw Fred and his mother.

"I came downtown to get clothes," said Fred. "I am larger than I was, and I had to get new clothes."

"I am larger than I was, and I had to have new clothes, too," said Sue.

"Now both of us are ready for school next week," said Fred.

ON THE WAY

The first day of the next week
all the children started back to school.
Some of them walked, and others rode
on the school bus.

Fred and Sue walked to school. "I am
happy that school is starting again,"
said Sue. "I like school."

"I like school, too," said Fred,
"and I am happy to start again."

Soon Fred and Sue came to a corner.
They looked to the left and to the right.

"There are no cars coming," said Sue,
"so it is safe for us to cross."

Fred and Sue came to another corner where there was a stop light.

"Look," said Fred. "The stop light is red, so we must wait."

Soon the light turned to green. "Now we may go," said Sue. "The light tells us that we will be safe."

Joe and Mary rode on a bus to school.
The bus came right by the house.

"Good morning, Mr. Jones," they said
to the man who ran the bus.

"Good morning," said Mr. Jones. "I am
glad to see you again."

Then Joe and Mary found good places
to sit on the bus.

Joe sat next to Bob, and Mary sat
next to Peggy on the bus. They talked
with Bob and Peggy, but did not walk
around. None of the children got up
to walk around in the bus.

By and by the bus came to a corner
where there was a policeman. He made
the bus stop so that people could cross
the street. Then he let the bus go
on its way down the street.

Soon the bus came to the schoolyard,
and the boys and girls got out.
They did not run or push or shout.

"There is Fred," said Joe.

"There is Sue," said Mary.

"Let us talk with them," said Joe.

Joe and Mary went over to talk
with Fred and Sue. They were happy
to see Fred and Sue again. Soon it was
time to go inside.

Tell or Show

How did you get ready to start to school this year?

What are safe ways to cross streets?

What are safe ways to ride in buses?

16

FOLLOW THE LEADER

All the children in the room liked
Miss Jackson. She had a soft voice,
and she was always kind. She helped
the boys and girls in many ways.

Sometimes she let the children play
games after they did their work.
Now and then, she told stories. She made
school seem like fun.

One day Miss Jackson took everyone
outdoors to play on the playground.
"What do you want to play?" she asked.

"Let's play Follow the Leader,"
said the children.

Jim was the first leader. He did
a duck walk. He did an elephant walk.
He jumped up high. He sat down.
All the children followed him.

18

Sue was the next leader. She danced
on one foot. She stood still. Then
she jumped and waved her arms.

All the children followed her.
They had fun playing the game.

CLEANING UP

The boys and girls got their hands dirty while playing outside. They went to the washrooms to wash their hands. Then they went back to their room.

Miss Jackson looked at their hands and said, "Some of you have washed your hands well, and others have not. Don, will you tell us how you washed your hands in the washroom?"

"First of all I put both my hands
under running water," said Don. "Next
I put soap on my hands and washed
one hand with the other. Then I put
them under running water once more
to wash off all the soap."

"Did you dry your hands well, Don?"
asked Miss Jackson.

"Yes, I tried to dry them well,"
said Don. "There were no dirty spots
on the towel. My hands were clean."

"Don's hands are clean," said Sue,
"but his arms are still dirty."

"Oh!" said Don. "I forgot to wash
my arms. I'll go and wash them."

After Don went to the washroom,
Miss Jackson said, "We should wash
our hands many times a day."

"I always wash my hands before I eat
any kind of food," said Mary.

"I always wash my hands after going
to the toilet," said Joe.

Just then Don came back to the room.
He put out his arms and said,
"This time I washed the right way."

What kinds of things do you like to do when you play Follow the Leader?

What other games do you like to play with the boys and girls at school?

How do you wash your hands?

When do you wash your hands?

24

LUNCH AT SCHOOL

Joe and Mary brought their lunches to school. Miss Jackson always brought her lunch to school, too.

One day Joe said, "Good! It is time for lunch. I'm always hungry when it is time for lunch."

Joe, Mary, and Miss Jackson went to wash their hands. Then they sat down at a table to eat.

Joe opened his lunch box. He had
a peanut butter sandwich, cookies,
and a big red apple. He had milk
to drink. Joe had a good lunch.

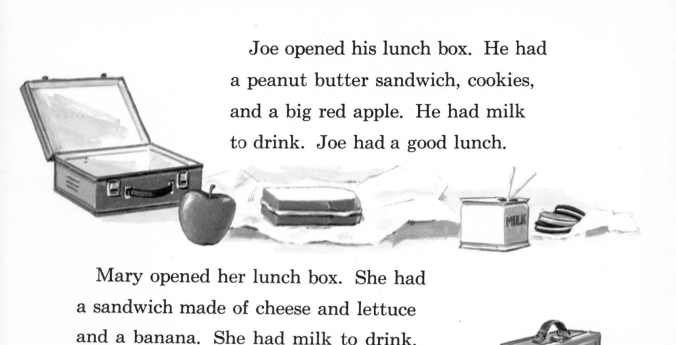

Mary opened her lunch box. She had
a sandwich made of cheese and lettuce
and a banana. She had milk to drink.
Mary had a good lunch.

Miss Jackson opened her lunch box.
She had a meat sandwich and an orange.
Also she had pieces of carrot. She had
some milk to drink.

Miss Jackson said to Joe and Mary,
"Would you like some carrot?"

"Yes, please," said the children.

"I have never had any carrot before,"
said Joe. "I would like to eat some
to see what it is like."

Joe ate some of the carrot. He ate
some more. "This is good," he said.
"I have found something new to eat.
It's fun to eat new foods."

Joe, Mary, and Miss Jackson went
for a walk after lunch. They stopped
at a water fountain. Joe wanted to get
a drink of water.

"How much water should we drink
every day?" asked Mary.

"Drink as much water as you wish,"
said Miss Jackson. "Some people need
more water than others."

THE FIRE DRILL

The boys and girls learned many things about their school. They learned to know where all the doors were. They found out what doors to use.

The children learned what to do when there was a fire drill at school. They learned how they should walk out when they heard the fire bell.

29

One morning there was a fire drill,
and all the children left their room.
They walked quickly down the steps
and out to the playground. They were
very quiet. They didn't start to run,
and they didn't talk.

"You did well in the fire drill,"
Miss Jackson said later. "I was
very proud of you."

"Yes, you did well," said Mr. White,
a fireman, who had been watching.
"I was very proud of you, too."

Tell or Show

What new foods have you tried lately?

How can you learn to like new foods?

Where do you drink water at school?

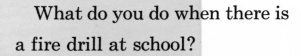

What do you do when there is
a fire drill at school?

32

DAY BY DAY

TOOTHBRUSHES

One morning Miss Jackson said,
"Let's talk about toothbrushes today.
Does everyone have a toothbrush?"

All the children in school said
that they had toothbrushes.

"I have two toothbrushes," said Bill.
"One is red, and the other is green."

"Why do you have two toothbrushes,
Bill?" asked Sue.

"I use my red toothbrush to brush
my teeth after breakfast," said Bill.
"I use my green toothbrush to brush
them after dinner.

"I always wash each toothbrush well
after I brush my teeth."

FOODS FOR BREAKFAST

"What foods do you like to eat
for breakfast?" asked Miss Jackson.
Everyone talked at once.

"I like oatmeal," said Sue.

"I like an orange or a grapefruit
and some bacon and eggs," said Bill.

"I like some corn flakes and bananas
and toast," said Jim.

"I like some orange juice, pancakes,
and milk," said Fred.

"You have named many good foods
for breakfast," said Miss Jackson.
"Let's put down the names of the foods
so that we may talk about them."

The children named the foods again,
and Miss Jackson put down the names.

"We have named many kinds of food,"
said Ruth. "Some like one kind of food,
and some like another."

milk   grapefruit
cocoa   orange juice
eggs   bananas
bacon
    oatmeal
    corn flakes
    toast

37

"What kinds of foods have you named?"
asked Miss Jackson.

"We have named fruits," said Sue.
"Oranges, bananas, and grapefruit are
kinds of fruit."

Miss Jackson asked, "What other kinds
of foods have you named?"

"We have named cereals," said Joe.
"Corn flakes and oatmeal are cereals."

"Fruits and cereals are good foods
for breakfast," said Miss Jackson,
"but there are other good foods."

"Milk is good," said Sue.

"Eggs and bacon are good," said Bill.

"Yes, there are many good foods
for breakfast," said Miss Jackson.

39

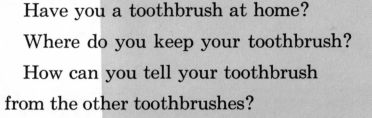

Have you a toothbrush at home?

Where do you keep your toothbrush?

How can you tell your toothbrush

from the other toothbrushes?

What kinds of foods do you like to eat

for breakfast in the morning?

40

SHORT AND TALL

One morning Bob and Joe asked
Miss Jackson about growing. "I am
just as old as Joe is," said Bob,
"but we do not grow alike. He is tall,
and I am short."

"Yes, Bob is just as old as I am,"
said Joe, "but we do not grow alike.
He is short, and I am tall."

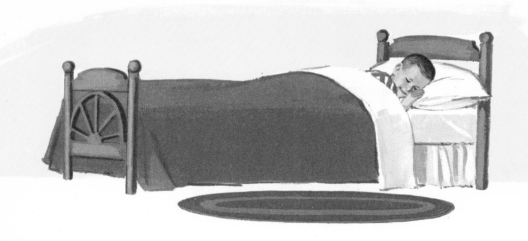

"I want to grow tall," said Bob.
"What can I do to grow tall?"

"Do you eat good foods for growing?"
asked Miss Jackson. "Do you always go
to bed on time?"

"Yes, I do," said Bob. "I drink milk
and eat other good foods. I go
to bed early every night."

"Children do not grow alike, Bob,"
said Miss Jackson. "Some grow more
in one year than other children do.
This year Joe has grown very fast,
and next year, you may grow fast."

"I hope so," said Bob. "I want
to become as tall as Joe."

"You must remember another thing,
Bob," said Miss Jackson. "Sometimes
children grow to be tall or short
like their fathers and mothers."

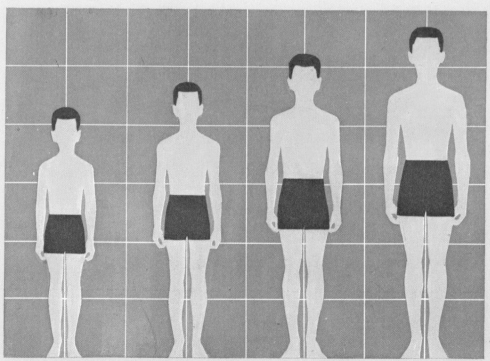

7 YEARS   10 YEARS   13 YEARS   16 YEARS

"My father is very tall," said Joe,
"and I am growing tall. Sometime
I may be as tall as he is."

"Both my father and my mother are
short," said Bob. "Now I am short,
too, but I am well."

"You may be short and still be
well and strong," said Miss Jackson.
"In the same way, Joe may be tall
and be well and strong, too."

44

SEEING AND HEARING

One morning Miss Jackson said,
"Today we will find out how well
all of you can see."

"How will we find out?" asked Jim.

"You will look at this big card
to find out," answered Miss Jackson.
"You will need to stand back and tell
what letters you see. Some letters are
big, and some are little."

Miss Jackson gave Fred a little piece
of paper. "Now cover one eye and read
with the other eye," she said.

Fred covered one eye at a time
and read all the letters.

Each boy and girl had a turn.

Ruth had glasses. She read well
with her glasses, but could not see
without her glasses. "My glasses help
me very much," she said.

When Ted's turn came, he couldn't see the little letters on the chart.

"I will talk with your mother, Ted," said Miss Jackson. "Then she can take you to see an eye doctor."

47

A week later, Ted had new glasses.
"Now I can see well," he said.

"Good!" said Miss Jackson.

The next day Miss Jackson said,
"Each of you will go to see Miss Gray,
the school nurse. She will find out
how well you can hear."

Miss Gray found that everyone
in the room could hear well.

Tell or Show

Why are some boys and girls tall
and other boys and girls short?

What can you do day by day to help
you grow and be strong?

How do you care for your eyes?
How do you care for your ears?

49

MARY'S COLD

One morning when Mary got up she had
a bad cold. Her head and eyes hurt,
and her nose ran.

"You cannot go to school with a cold,"
said her mother.

Mary knew that her mother was right,
so she stayed in bed most of the day.
She rested quietly. She ate good food
and had water and milk to drink.

By late afternoon Mary was better.

She began to play with her dolls.

After school Peggy stopped to ask
why Mary was not in school.

"She has a cold, but she is better,"
said her mother. "Thank you for coming."

Mary went to the doorway and said,
"Don't come into my room, Peggy.
You might get my cold."

The next day, Peggy told Miss Jackson
that Mary had a cold.

"That is too bad," said Miss Jackson,
"but I'm glad that she stayed at home
this morning. Now you will not catch
a cold from her. When children have
colds, they should stay at home."

A SURPRISE FOR BETH

Beth's father said, "I have a surprise for you. Can you guess what it is?"

"Is it a doll?" asked Beth.

"No, it is not," answered Father.

"Is it a ball?" asked Beth.

"No, it is not," answered Father.

"Is it a book?" asked Beth.

"No, it is not," answered Father again.

53

"I can't guess," said Beth. "Please tell me what it is."

Father gave Beth a basket and said, "Your surprise is a kitten."

Beth took off the top of the basket and looked inside. There before her was a pretty white kitten.

"What will you name your kitten?"
asked Father.

"She is so white that I'll name her
Snowflake," answered Beth.

Snowflake was very clean. She washed
herself many times a day.

"She washes herself many more times
than I wash myself," said Beth.

A BAD DAY FOR DON

One night Don stayed up to watch
a TV show. The next morning he got up
late and couldn't eat breakfast.

At school that day he almost went
to sleep. He couldn't do his work
well. At last he splashed paint
on Jane's pretty dress.

After school Bill asked Don to play with him for a while.

"I am too tired to play with you this afternoon," said Don.

"Why are you tired?" asked Bill.

"I stayed up late last night to see a TV show," said Don. "I did not get enough sleep."

This was a bad day for Don.

Tell or Show

Why should you always stay at home
when you have a cold?

Do you think that Beth's kitten washed
itself more than Beth washed herself?
How often do you wash yourself?

What happens to you if you don't get
enough sleep and rest?

58

WORK AND PLAY

SAFETY AT WORK

One morning Bill came to school
with a white bandage on his hand.

"How did you hurt your hand, Bill?"
asked Miss Jackson.

"I cut my hand with a little saw
while making something," said Bill.

"What happened?" asked Miss Jackson.
"Tell us what you did."

"I was cutting some large pieces
of wood into little pieces," said Bill.
"Soon I heard something and looked up
for a minute. Then the saw jumped
and cut my hand."

"My father said that we should be
careful when we work with tools,"
said Fred. "Tools can hurt us."

"I hurt my hand once with a hammer,"
said Don. "Now whenever I need to use
a hammer, I'm very careful."

"I fell over a hammer once and hurt
myself," said Beth. "My brother forgot
to put the hammer back in the box
after he stopped using it."

"We must always be careful with tools,"
said Miss Jackson. "We must always put
them away after we stop work."

SAFETY AT PLAY

"We have just talked about safety at work," said Miss Jackson. "Let's talk about safety at play. How do you keep safe when you play?"

"I like to climb trees," said Joe. "Whenever I climb, I always hold on with both hands while I move my feet. I never let go with both of my hands at the same time."

63

"Joe and I sometimes play together," said Bruce, "but we always play in safe places. We never play games out in the street."

"I like to skate, but I always stay on the sidewalk," said Carol. "I watch for people backing out in their cars. I take off my skates whenever I cross the street, so that I won't fall."

64

Peggy said, "Mary and I like to cut
dolls out of paper with our scissors.
We try to be very careful when we cut
with the scissors."

"We always put away the scissors
after we stop using them," said Mary.

"Yes, you need to be very careful
with scissors," said Miss Jackson.
"Be careful with anything that cuts."

65

Tell or Show

How can you be safe in using
saws, hammers, and other tools?
What should you do with tools
when you stop using them?

How do you keep safe when you play?
Where are some safe places to play
near your home?

STRANGE ANIMALS

One day a big dog ran up to Ruth
on her way to school. She walked on
and did not stop to pet the dog.
Soon the dog left.

When Ruth got to school, she told
Miss Jackson and the other children
about the dog. Then all of them began
to talk about strange animals.

"Ruth was right in not stopping
to pet the strange dog," said Bill.

"Some dogs don't like strange people,"
said Joe. "My dog doesn't."

"My cat doesn't like strange people,"
said Sue. "She runs from them."

CAPTAIN

68

"My father said that I should stay away from strange animals," said Jim.

"Yes, strange animals may hurt you," said Miss Jackson. "Always play only with animals that you know.

"Just as you should always stay away from strange animals, you should stay away from strange people. Never get into a car or go with anyone strange."

FARM ANIMALS

Bob lived on a farm. One day he told the boys and girls about the farm.

"My father keeps many cows," he said. "The cows are big. Most of them are black and white."

"What do the cows eat?" asked Sue.

"They eat green grass in the summer and hay in the winter," said Bob. "They drink much water, too."

"Where do the cows stay?" asked Fred.

"They stay in a big field sometimes and in a barn sometimes," said Bob. "Each cow has a place in the barn."

"Do the cows give milk?" asked Don.

"Yes," said Bob. "My father milks them two times a day. He milks them every morning and every night. I help him to keep the barn clean."

"What other animals do you have
on the farm?" asked Bruce.

"We have some pigs and chickens,"
answered Bob. "I always feed the pigs,
and my sister feeds the chickens.
Both of us go to the chicken house
to get eggs every day."

"I think it would be fun to live
on a farm," said Jim.

Tell or Show

Why is it safe to play with your pets, but not with strange animals?

What farm animals have you seen?

What farm animals do you like best?

What good foods do you eat that come from cows and chickens?

One day Miss Jackson went outdoors
to play with the children. "I want
to show you a new game," she said.

"What is the game?" asked Sue.

"The game is called a relay race,"
answered Miss Jackson.

Then Miss Jackson made two lines
for the children to use. The lines were
across the playground from each other.

"Now we will make up two teams
to play the game," said Miss Jackson.
"The boys and girls on one team will race
those on the other team."

She asked players from both teams
to get back of the lines. Then they waited
for the race to start.

Soon she put up her hand and let it
fall quickly. "Go," she shouted.

The first player on each team ran
to the line across the playground.
He put his hand on the first player
on his team behind the line.

That player ran back to the first line
and put his hand on the next player
on his team.

The race went on until one team used
all of its players.

The children ran fast in the race,
but they were careful not to run
into one another.

"You played very hard, but you were
careful," said Miss Jackson.

The children liked the relay race,
and everyone had fun.

A GAME OF TAG

One morning Miss Jackson showed
the children a new way to play tag.
She made two lines a little way
from each other on the playground.

"Now we can start to play," she said.
"All of you stand on one line, ready
to run to the other line."

Joe was It and stood in a place
to catch some of the children.
He called, "Come over, Rover."

The children ran to the other line,
and Joe tried to tag some of them.
He got Mary and Bob. Then they began
to help Joe tag the others.

Joe called again, "Come over, Rover."

The children ran to the first line
again. Joe, Mary, and Bob ran to tag
the children.

The game went on until there were
no more children to tag.

Tell or Show

What do you do in a relay race?

What tag games do you play at school?

What games do you know that are best
for three or four children to play?

What games do you know that are best
for many children to play?

KEEPING WELL

PEGGY AND THE DENTIST

Peggy's mother came into the bedroom
when Peggy was going to bed. "Tomorrow
I want to take you to see Dr. Green,
the dentist," she said.

Peggy liked Dr. Green. She went to see
him two times a year. He helped her
to take good care of her teeth.

The next day after Peggy came home
from school, she and her mother went
downtown on a bus. In a little while
they got off and walked to the building
where Dr. Green worked.

Dr. Green looked at Peggy's teeth,
and cleaned them. He found a small hole
in one of her teeth. Then he cleaned
the hole and filled it.

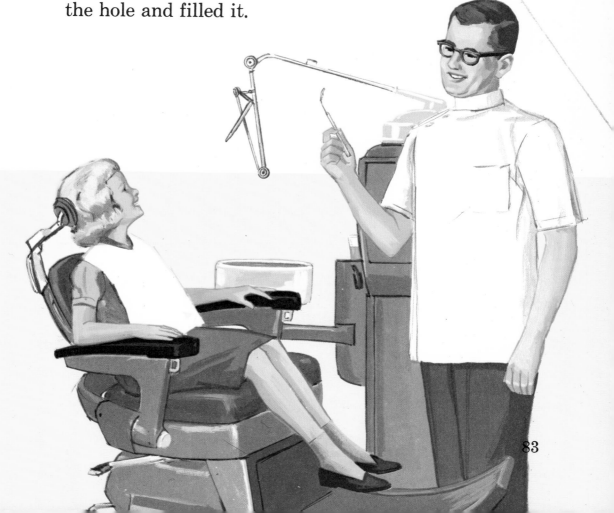

HOW MANY TEETH?

One afternoon Miss Jackson asked, "Which of you can bring small mirrors to school tomorrow?"

All of the children looked surprised, but said that they would bring mirrors. The next day every child came to school with a mirror.

"Now, you may use the mirrors to look at your teeth," said Miss Jackson. "Open your mouths and look."

The boys and girls opened their mouths to look at their teeth. They had to look hard to see all their teeth.

"Look to see just how many teeth
you have," said Miss Jackson.

The children found that some had
more teeth than others.

"May I put down our names and show
how many teeth we have?" asked Fred.

"Yes, let me see how many teeth
you have," said Miss Jackson.

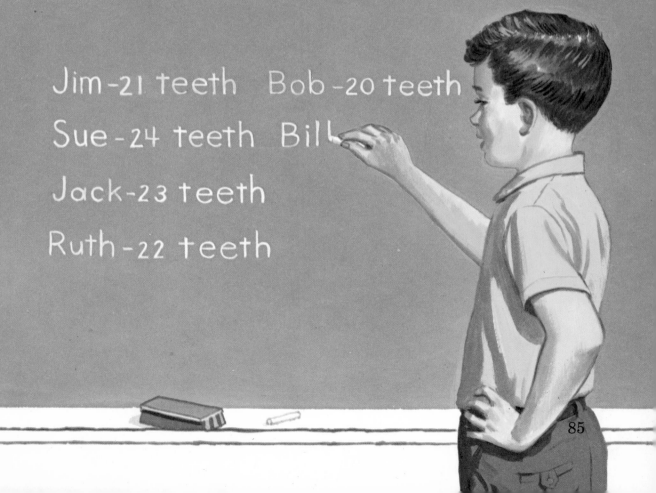

Jim-21 teeth Bob-20 teeth
Sue-24 teeth Bill
Jack-23 teeth
Ruth-22 teeth

Miss Jackson next asked the children to look in their mirrors and to make pictures of their teeth.

The children started to make pictures and found that their front teeth were not like their back teeth. "Our teeth are not alike," said Fred.

"That is right," said Miss Jackson. "Whenever you eat something, you need to use some of your teeth for biting and others for chewing."

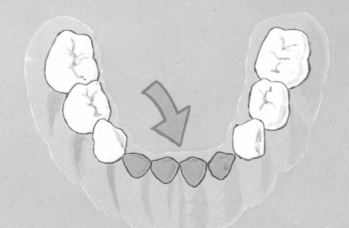

LOWER TEETH USED FOR BITING

"I use my front teeth for biting," said Bob, looking in the mirror.

"I use my back teeth for chewing," said Ruth.

"Yes, your front teeth are good for biting, and your back teeth are good for chewing," said Miss Jackson.

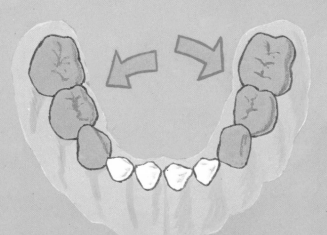

LOWER TEETH USED FOR CHEWING

"I lost my front teeth," said Ed. "Now I can't bite very well."

"You'll soon get other teeth to take their place," said Miss Jackson. "Then you can bite well again."

"Yes, the teeth that I lost were baby teeth," said Ed. "Soon I'll get some permanent teeth."

"You will need your permanent teeth for a long time," said Miss Jackson. "You must take care of them."

MAKING TOOTH POWDER

One afternoon the children wanted
something new to do. They asked what
they might do for a while.

"I know of something you might do,"
said Miss Jackson. "You can learn
to make tooth powder."

Miss Jackson got out a box of salt
and a box of baking soda. She put
the salt and soda on a table.

Some of the children came to help
Miss Jackson make the powder.

SALT

BAKING
SODA

89

Miss Jackson watched the children. She told them how much salt to use and how much baking soda to use.

Bob put the salt and baking soda together in a cup. After a little while the tooth powder was ready.

"You can make tooth powder like this, or you can buy tooth powder at a store," said Miss Jackson. "Some people like toothpaste better than tooth powder."

"I like toothpaste," said Jim.

"In caring for our teeth we must be sure that we know how to brush them," said Miss Jackson. "Will someone tell how to brush teeth?"

"I brush down on my upper teeth, and up on my lower teeth," said Peggy. "I brush my teeth both inside and out, and I brush the tops."

"I brush my teeth in the same way," said Don. "When I get home I'll make some tooth powder for brushing them."

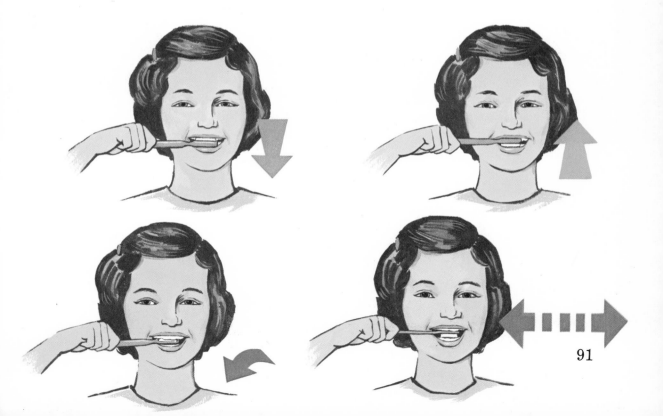

91

Tell or Show

What does the dentist do for you?

When do you go to see your dentist?

How many teeth have you now?

Which teeth do you use for biting?

Which teeth do you use for chewing?

How can you make tooth powder?

DUST IN THE SUNLIGHT

Bright sunlight came into the room
through the window. Jim moved
a little to keep the bright sunlight
away from his book.

"I see little pieces of something
in the sunlight," said Jim. "They seem
to dance about. What are they?"

"Pieces of dust," said Miss Jackson.
"There are always little pieces of dust
in the air, but we can only see them
in bright light."

93

Jim sneezed and didn't have time
to cover his nose and mouth.

"When someone sneezes like that
the air all around him becomes filled
with bits of water," said Miss Jackson.

"I cannot see the bits of water,
but I know that they left my nose
and mouth," said Jim.

"There may be germs in the bits of water from Jim's nose and mouth," said Miss Jackson.

"Are there any germs in the pieces of dust that I saw?" asked Jim.

"Yes," said Miss Jackson. "There are germs in the air. Those which come from people's noses and mouths can give us colds and other diseases."

"What can you do to keep germs
out of the air when you sneeze?"
asked Miss Jackson.

"We can cover our noses and mouths
when we sneeze," said Fred. "Then
the germs can't get into the air."

"That is right," said Miss Jackson.
"If we remember to cover our noses
and mouths, we can keep from giving
germs to other people."

THE TWO PUPPIES

One morning Bill looked at a plant
at school. "See how it is growing,"
he said to Miss Jackson.

"Yes, many things around you grow,"
said Miss Jackson. "Plants grow
and animals grow. You grow, too."

"Why do some boys and girls grow more than others?" asked Don.

"Let me answer by telling a story," said Miss Jackson. "Once there were two little puppies that were brothers. One of the puppies was named Buck, and the other was named Pepper.

"When the puppies were six weeks old, they were given away. Buck was given to a boy who lived in the country. The boy lived on a farm.

"Pepper was given to a girl who lived in a big city."

"Buck liked the country. Every day
he and the boy played on the farm.
They played until they were tired.
Then they rested.

"Buck had milk to drink every day,
and he had other good foods to eat.
He grew very fast."

99

"Pepper, who lived in the city, had
to stay indoors almost all the time.
He played only in the house.

"There were no good places outdoors
where he could play. There was no yard
around the house.

"Pepper didn't have very good foods
to eat. Sometimes the girl forgot
to feed him. She never once gave
him milk to drink."

"When the puppies were one year old,
Buck was much larger and stronger
than Pepper. Then, as you might guess,
he was much happier than Pepper."

"I guess that we are like puppies,"
said Beth. "We need to eat good foods.
We need to play outdoors and to get
much sleep and rest. Then we can grow
and be strong and happy."

Tell or Show

Why can't you see germs?

How may germs hurt people?

Why should you cover your nose
and mouth when you sneeze?

Why did Buck grow better than Pepper?

Are you larger and stronger this year
than you were last year?

HELP FROM OTHERS

Bob was trying to color a picture,
but he had to stop. His neck began
to hurt. His head was hot.

"You must go to see Miss Gray,
the school nurse," said Miss Jackson.

Bob went to see Miss Gray. He told
her that his neck hurt.

Miss Gray told Bob to sit down,
and put a thermometer in his mouth.
"First of all we need to find out
if you have a fever," she said.

In a short time Miss Gray took
the thermometer from Bob's mouth.
Then she looked at it.

"Yes, you have a fever," she said,
"so you must go home. I will talk
with your mother."

Bob stayed with the school nurse
until his mother came to get him.

When Bob got home, his mother put
him to bed. Then she called Dr. Lane
on the telephone.

Doctor Lane came to Bob's house
to see him. Bob liked Doctor Lane.
They were good friends.

Doctor Lane looked at Bob's eyes,
and he looked in Bob's mouth. He put
a thermometer in Bob's mouth to see
if he had a fever.

"I'm afraid you'll have to stay
in bed for a while, Bob," he said.
"You are sick with the mumps."

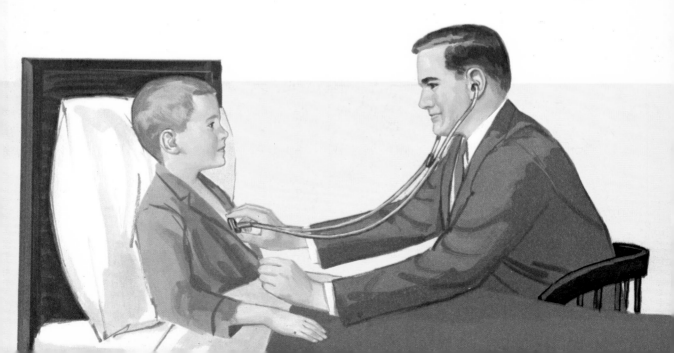

Bob had to stay at home for a while
with the mumps. He missed his school.
He missed seeing his friends. He missed
seeing Miss Jackson.

One day Bob's mother brought him
a letter. It came from Miss Jackson
and the boys and girls at school.

The letter made Bob happy. He knew
that everyone at school missed him
as much as he missed them.

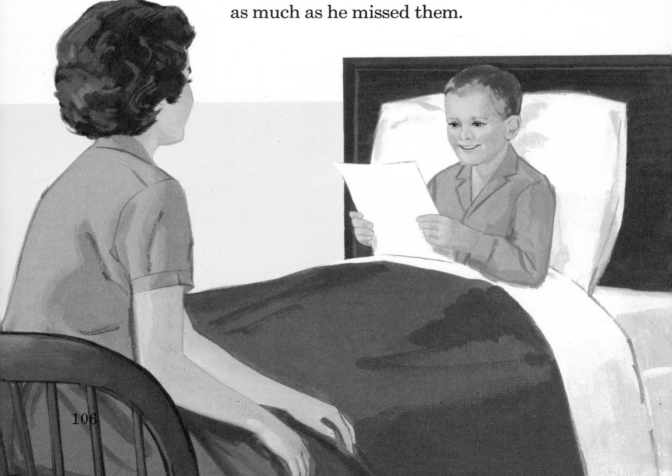

Bob got a letter ready to send
to Miss Jackson and the children.
Everyone at school was very happy
to hear from him.

Dear Friends,
Thank you for your
letter. You helped
me to get well.
I feel much better
now. I will be back
in school soon.
                Bob

"We are glad that Bob is better,"
said Miss Jackson.

By and by Bob was well and came
back to school. "Many people helped
me while I had mumps," he said.
"Miss Gray and Doctor Lane helped me,
and my mother and you helped me."

Tell or Show

Who helped Bob when he was sick?

How did Miss Gray help?

How did Dr. Lane help?

How did Bob's mother help?

How did Miss Jackson help?

108   Who helps you when you are sick?

TOGETHER

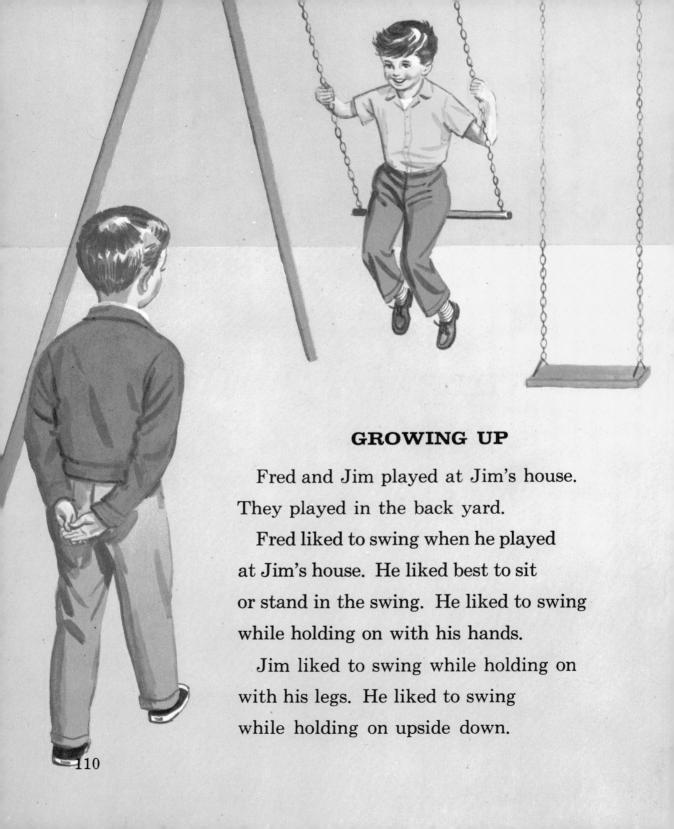

GROWING UP

Fred and Jim played at Jim's house.
They played in the back yard.

Fred liked to swing when he played
at Jim's house. He liked best to sit
or stand in the swing. He liked to swing
while holding on with his hands.

Jim liked to swing while holding on
with his legs. He liked to swing
while holding on upside down.

Jim and Fred had fun. They sat down when they got tired. Jim's mother gave them some fruit juice to drink.

She watched the boys drink the juice. Then she said, "You boys are growing. You are much larger than you were."

"Fred is much larger, and I am much larger, too," said Jim.

"Both of you boys are much larger than you were," said Jim's mother.

"At school Miss Jackson told us that we are growing in many ways," said Fred. "She said that we are larger than we were and that we do many more things."

"I know that I do many more things than I did," said Jim.

"Yes, I can tell," said Jim's mother. "You do many more things to help at home. You help to clean the house, and you help to wash the car."

"I help at home, too," said Fred.
"I go to the store for my mother,
and I put tools away for my father.
Last week I helped to build a house
for my dog, Corky."

"You do as many things at home
as I do," said Jim.

DAN AND HIS FATHER

One day Dan's father began to cut the grass in the yard. He worked hard to cut the grass.

"Let me help you," called Dan. "I will clean up the grass and put it into a big basket."

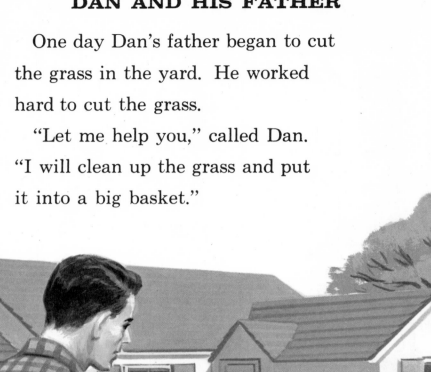

Dan worked hard in the yard.
He cleaned up the grass and put it
into a large basket. Soon he had
the basket full. His father came
to carry the basket away.

"Thank you for coming to help
me, Dan," said his father.

A short time later, Dan was playing
outdoors with his wagon. All at once
a wheel came off.

Dan tried hard to put on the wheel,
but it kept coming off.

At last Dan went to his father
and said, "A wheel came off my wagon.
Will you come to put it on?"

"Let me see the wheel," said Father.
"I will be glad to help."

116

Soon Dan's father had put the wheel
back on the wagon. "Now my wagon is
just as good as it was," said Dan.
"Thank you for helping me."

"That was fun," said Dan's father.
"You helped me clean up the grass,
and I helped you put on the wheel.
It's fun to help each other."

Tell or Show

In what ways are you growing?

How can you show your mother and father that you are growing?

How do you help others in your family and how do they help you?

TALKING THINGS OVER

One night Bill's father asked Bill to go down to the workroom to get him a hammer. Bill was afraid to go down to the workroom in the dark. "Do I have to go?" he asked.

"Are you afraid?" asked his father.

"Yes, I am afraid," answered Bill. "I don't like dark places."

"We will go down to the workroom together," said Bill's father.

Then Bill and his father went down to the workroom together. They turned on the light. They looked all around. Bill got the hammer.

"I am not afraid in the workroom when the light is on," said Bill.

"Everyone is afraid now and then,"
said Bill's father. "Being afraid
helps to make us careful."

Bill and his father went up again.

"Sometimes, when we know about a thing,
we are not afraid of it," said Father.
"Be sure to tell your mother or me
whenever you are afraid of anything.
We can help you, Bill."

121

TAKING TURNS

Sometimes Bob, Gary, and Joe played
ball together. Bob threw the ball
with his right hand, and Joe threw it
with his left hand.

Bob and Joe threw the ball better
than Gary threw it. They took turns
being pitcher when they played.

One day Bob said, "Why don't we let Gary be pitcher once in a while?"

"I think we should," answered Joe. "Let's all three take turns being pitcher from now on."

From then on when the boys played ball, all three of them took turns being pitcher. Gary learned to pitch almost as well as the other boys. Then everyone had fun.

Tell or Show

Does being afraid help sometimes?

Do you talk things over with someone
when you are afraid?

How can you help others

when you play games?

Why should you take turns?

LEARNING ABOUT FIRE

One morning Miss Jackson asked
the children how they used fire
to help them at home. "How do you use
fire at home?" she asked.

"We use fire at home to help keep
our house warm," said Jim.

"My father uses fire for burning
leaves from the yard," said Fred.

"My mother uses fire for getting
foods ready to eat," said Amy.

"We have talked about good things
that fire does," said Miss Jackson.
"Now let us talk about bad things
that fire does."

"Fire can burn things," said Ruth.
"It can burn houses and other buildings,
and it can burn people."

"My mother said that I should keep
away from fire," said Joe. "She told
me not to play with fire."

126

"What would you do if you found
that your clothes had caught fire?"
asked Miss Jackson.

"I would hurry to put a blanket
or a coat around me," said Joe.

"I would get down fast on the floor
or ground and roll over," said Sue.

"Sometimes a fire starts outdoors
in woods or dry grass," said Fred.

127

"When we build a fire somewhere
outdoors, my father always is careful
to put it out," said Mark. "He said
that fire is a good friend, if we use
it in the right way."

"Yes, fire can be very good for us
or bad for us," said Peggy.

"I'm afraid of fire, so I stay away
from it," said Gary.

"I'm afraid of fire, too," said Sue,
"and I'm very careful around it."

"Being afraid of fire helps to make
you careful," said Miss Jackson.

AN EGGNOG PARTY

One afternoon Miss Jackson asked, "Do you children like eggnog?"

The children said that they liked eggnog very much. "My mother makes eggnog," said Sue. "She makes it almost every week."

"Would you like to make eggnog here at school?" asked Miss Jackson.

"Oh, making eggnog would be fun," cried the children.

Miss Jackson asked three children
to come and help her. They washed
their hands and came to the table
at the front of the room.

First Miss Jackson put a big bowl
on the table before the children. Then
she got eggs, milk, and other things
for making the eggnog.

130

The children helped Miss Jackson
put things in the bowl. She told them
which things to put in the bowl first
and which to put in next.

She told the children just how much
of everything to put in the bowl.
"We must have enough of everything,
but not too much," she said.

By and by the eggnog was ready
for the children to drink.

Miss Jackson had the children come
to the table one by one. She gave
each of them a big paper cup filled
with eggnog.

All the children liked the eggnog.
"Thank you, Miss Jackson," they said.

"I am going to ask my mother to let
me make some eggnog at home tonight
for my sister and me," said Bill.

THE HOBBY SHOW

"We are going to have a hobby show at school," Jane said to her mother. "I wish that I could take something to the show."

"Well, what would you like to take?" asked her mother.

"I would like to take my bowl of fish to the show," said Jane. "That would be the best thing there."

"You can't be sure," said her mother. "The other children may want to bring good things to the show, too."

Jane took her bowl of fish to school for the show. Jim brought a big box filled with pretty stones. Sue brought a picture book that she had made.

Some of the girls brought small dolls and doll dresses. Beth brought dolls dressed in many colors.

"You were right, Mother," said Jane
that night. "The other children brought
good things from home, too. I liked
all the things, but I still like
my bowl of fish best."

Tell or Show

How does fire help people at home?

Why is fire sometimes bad for people?

What would you do if you found

that your clothes were on fire?

How can you make eggnog at home?

What other good things are made

from milk and eggs?

What did Jane learn at the hobby show?

HELPING OTHERS

MOTHER'S HELPER

Peggy liked to help her mother do things at home. "I like to help you, Mother," she said.

"You help me in many ways, Peggy," said her mother. "You help me to get the table ready for dinner. You help me to make the beds."

"Are there other things that I may do
to help you?" asked Peggy.

Then Peggy's mother smiled and said,
"You can come to breakfast on time,
and you can put away your clothes.
You can pick up your toys."

"Yes, I can," said Peggy. "I will do
those things for you, too."

MANY HELPERS

Mary and her brother Roger helped
their mother to get dinner.

Mary helped her mother to do things
in the kitchen. She helped to get out
foods for her mother, and she helped
to clean carrots.

"Thank you for helping me get dinner
tonight," said Mother. "It was fun
for us to work together."

"How many people helped to get dinner
tonight?" asked Father.

"Mother, Roger, and I helped to get
dinner," answered Mary.

"Many other people helped to get
dinner, too, but you didn't think
of them," said Father.

"Oh, I know who helped," said Roger. "A farmer took care of cows and milked the cows. A milkman brought the milk to our house."

"Someone made the butter," said Mary, "and someone grew the vegetables."

"Someone grew the fruits and made the bread," said Father.

"Someone made the table and chairs that we are using, and someone made things in the kitchen," said Roger.

"You helped, too, Father," said Mary with a smile. "You helped us to get money for buying food."

Mary laughed. "Mother," she said, "many people besides Roger and me helped you get dinner tonight."

Tell or Show

There are many people who help you day after day. Who are these helpers and what do they do?

NEAT AND CLEAN

One day, some of the boys talked about keeping neat and clean.

"I take baths two or three times a week," said Mark. "I like to take baths at home."

"I take baths two or three times a week, too," said Dan. "I think it is fun to take baths."

"Sometimes I take a bath by putting water into a big pan," said Carl. "Then I wash myself with a wash cloth."

"I always use warm water for taking
baths," said Dan. "I like warm water
with soap for bathing."

"I always use warm water with soap,
too, for bathing," said Mark.

"I always use my own wash cloth
and towel for bathing," said Carl.

"So do I," said Dan.

"I use a small brush for cleaning my fingernails," said Dan. "I like to keep my fingernails clean."

"I use a brush for keeping my hair neat," said Carl.

"I brush my hair after I get up in the morning," said Mark. "I like to keep my hair neat."

"I have a shoe brush," said Dan.
"Every day or two I give my shoes
a good brushing."

"Sometimes I brush my clothes
to make them look neat and clean,"
said Carl. "I always put them away
when I take them off."

"I always put my clothes away,
too, when I take them off," said Mark.

"Putting clothes away helps to keep
them neat and clean," said Dan.

CLOTHES AND THE WEATHER

"Mother, what clothes should I wear to school tomorrow?" asked Amy.

"First let us try to find out what the weather will be like tomorrow," said her mother. "Then we can pick the right kind of clothes."

"We can watch TV to find out about the weather," said Amy.

"We can look at the paper, too, to find out," said her mother.

"We can look at the thermometer in the morning," said Amy.

"Yes, the thermometer will tell us just how hot or cold it is outside," said Amy's mother. "It will not tell anything about rain or snow."

Amy and her mother watched TV
to find out about the weather.

"It is going to rain," said Amy.
"Now what shall I wear?"

"You should wear your raincoat,
your rain hat, and your overshoes,"
said her mother. "They will help
to keep you dry in the rain."

Tell or Show

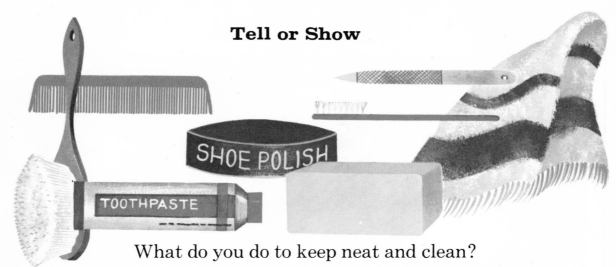

What do you do to keep neat and clean?

How do you know what clothes to wear?

WASHING FOOD

One morning Miss Jackson brought some celery and carrots to school.

"Are we going to eat the celery and carrots?" asked Bob.

"Yes, but we must get them ready to eat first," answered Miss Jackson. "What must we do first to get them ready to eat?"

"We must wash them," said Ruth.

"That is right," said Miss Jackson.
"Fred, Sue, and Jim, will you clean
the celery and carrots for us?"

The three children went to wash
their hands well. Then they began
to wash the celery and carrots.

Soon the celery and carrots were
clean and Miss Jackson began to cut
them into pieces. In a little while
the celery and carrots were ready
for the children to eat.

All the other children washed
their hands. They wanted to have
clean hands for eating.

Fred, Sue, and Jim began to take
the celery and carrots around the room.
Each boy and girl took pieces
and began to eat.

"Do you like celery and carrots?"
asked Miss Jackson.

"Oh, yes," answered the children.
"Thank you, Miss Jackson."

THE PICNIC

One morning Fred's mother said,
"Let's go on a picnic today."

"Let's go to Green Lake, where
we can swim," said Fred's father.
"Then we can rest and go for a walk
in the woods."

"You may ask some friends to go
with us, Fred," said his mother.

Fred asked Ruth, Jim, and Sue to go
along on the picnic.

Green Lake was pretty. The water was
clear. The sun was bright. There were
many green trees near the lake.

"When may we go swimming, Father?"
asked Fred.

"You may go swimming right now
if you wish," answered his father.
"You have time to swim before you eat."

Everyone wanted to swim.

"What can you do to be careful
while you swim?" asked Mr. Brown.

"We can stay with you," said Sue.
"You are big so you can watch us
while we swim."

"We can be careful not to push anyone
under water," said Ruth.

"We can come out of the water if we get
cold or tired," said Fred.

"All those are good things to do
while you swim," said Fred's father.

Fred's mother had lunch ready
to eat. She gave all the children
meat sandwiches, oranges, and milk.
Then in a little while she gave
them some ice cream.

After the children ate, they rested for a while. "Now may we take a walk in the woods?" asked Fred.

"First you must pick up the pieces of paper and food left from lunch," said his mother.

Fred and Jim picked up the pieces and put them into a big can.

WASTE

Everyone had a good time walking
in the woods. They saw and heard
many birds in the trees. Fred saw
a rabbit, and Sue saw a squirrel.

"We must be very quiet as we walk,
or the animals will be afraid of us,"
said Fred's father. "Let us walk
quietly through the woods."

The children tried to be quiet
from then on. They saw and heard
more birds in the trees. They saw
more rabbits and squirrels.

Fred's mother told the children
the names of the birds. She told
them how the birds lived.

"Wait, don't touch that plant
with three bright green leaves,"
called Fred's mother. "That plant is
poison ivy."

"I touched poison ivy one time,"
said Sue, "and I want to be careful
not to touch it again. It made
my skin red and sore."

"Now that we can tell poison ivy
when we see it, we can be careful
not to touch it," said Bill.

Ruth, Jim, and Sue thanked
Fred's father and mother for taking
them to the picnic.

"We had a good lunch," said Ruth.

"We liked to swim," said Jim.

"We liked to walk in the woods,"
said Sue. "All of us had fun."